Life As ...

Life As a Passenger on the *Mayflower*

Laura L. Sullivan

Cavendish Square

New York

Published in 2017 by Cavendish Square Publishing, LLC
243 5th Avenue, Suite 136, New York, NY 10016

Copyright © 2017 by Cavendish Square Publishing, LLC

First Edition

Library of Congress Cataloging-in-Publication Data
Names: Sullivan, Laura L., 1974- author.
Title: Life as a passenger on the Mayflower / Laura L. Sullivan.
Description: New York : Cavendish Square Publishing, 2016. | Series: Life as ... | Includes index.
Identifiers: LCCN 2016002180 (print) | LCCN 2016002852 (ebook) | ISBN 9781502617972 (pbk.) | ISBN 9781502617897 (library bound) | ISBN 9781502617675 (6 pack) | ISBN 9781502617781 (ebook)
Subjects: LCSH: Pilgrims (New Plymouth Colony)--Juvenile literature. | Mayflower (Ship)--Juvenile literature. | Massachusetts--History--New Plymouth, 1620-1691--Juvenile literature.
Classification: LCC F68 .S94 2016 (print) | LCC F68 (ebook) | DDC 974.4/02--dc23
LC record available at http://lccn.loc.gov/2016002180

Editorial Director: David McNamara
Editor: Kristen Susienka
Copy Editor: Rebecca Rohan
Art Director: Jeffrey Talbot
Designer: Alan Sliwinski
Production Assistant: Karol Szymczuk
Photo Research: J8 Media

The photographs in this book are used by permission and through the courtesy of:
Ann Ronan Pictures/Print Collector/Getty Images, cover; Time Life Pictures/Mansell/The LIFE Picture Collection/Getty Images, 5; The Protected Art Archive/Alamy Stock Photo, 6; James Edwin (1903-95)/Private Collection/© Look and Learn/Bridgeman Images, 9; Peter Ptschelinzew/Lonely Planet Images/Getty Images, 10; Jean Leon Gerome Ferris (1863–1930)/Library of Congress/File: The Mayflower Compact 1620 cph.3g07155.jpg/Wikimedia Commons, 13; McBride, Angus (1931-2007)/Private Collection/© Look and Learn/Bridgeman Images, 14; Wellcome Library, London/File: Ship's biscuit, England, 1875 Wellcome L0064860.jpg/Wikimedia Commons, 17; Irina Kovancova/Shutterstock.com, 19; De Agostini Picture Library/Getty Images, 20; Jonathon Potter/Getty Images, 22; Krista Rossow/National Geographic/Getty Images, 23; North Wind Picture Archives, 24; Jean Leon Gerome Ferris (1863–1930)/Library of Congress/File: The First Thanksgiving cph.3g04961.jpg/Wikimedia Commons, 26.

Printed in the United States of America

Contents

Introduction

In 1620, a group of people crossed the Atlantic Ocean in a ship called the *Mayflower*. The passengers were called **Pilgrims**. They traveled on the *Mayflower* for many reasons. In England, some Pilgrims were treated badly because of their religious beliefs. They left England to find a new place to practice their religion. Other passengers were farmers, servants, and families. When they arrived in America, which they called the New World, they faced many challenges.

Even though they were different, the passengers worked together to build a home. On the ship, they wrote an agreement to help each other.

This is the story of their journey.

The Pilgrims traveled to the New World aboard the *Mayflower*.

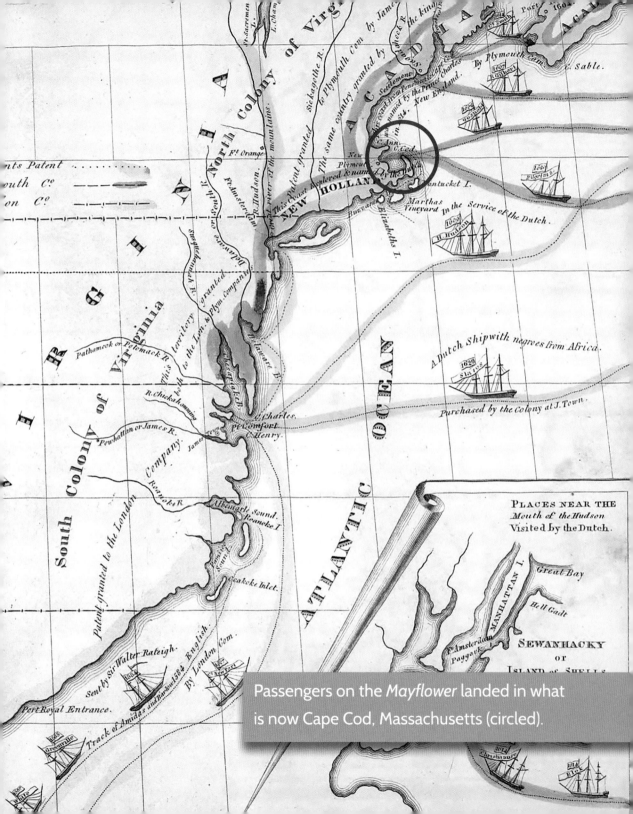

Passengers on the *Mayflower* landed in what is now Cape Cod, Massachusetts (circled).

Chapter 1

A Search for Religious Freedom

Some of the people who would become known as the Pilgrims were part of a religious group in England. Their ideas about religion were different from the official Church of England.

In the late 1500s and early 1600s, it was against the law to hold a service for any church other than the Church of England. Those who did could be put in prison, fined, or even killed. The religious group wanted the freedom to practice their own religion and hold their own services. They soon realized they had to move in order for that to happen.

First, the **congregation** moved to Leiden, Holland. That city let them worship as they wished. However, it was hard for them to live there. The city had different customs, and many people felt they had to abandon their "Englishness" to live there.

They decided to return to England and then travel to America to make a new home there. In the New World, they thought, they could make their

The *Speedwell*

Most people have heard of the *Mayflower*, but at the beginning of the journey there had been two ships. The *Speedwell* carried some of the Pilgrims and other passengers and crew. But almost as soon as the ships set sail from England, the *Speedwell* sprang a leak and had to stop traveling. One theory says the crew made the leak on purpose. They had second thoughts about the dangerous voyage.

The Pilgrims set sail from England with all of the supplies they thought they would need in their new home.

own decisions about how to live their lives. All of the congregation couldn't go at once. The youngest and strongest decided to go first. The others would follow later if they could. The first group set sail on the *Mayflower* in September 1620.

The *Mayflower* was crowded, and people slept on the floor or in hammocks.

Chapter 2
Saints and Strangers

Not all of the passengers on the *Mayflower* wanted religious freedom. In fact, only 37 of the 102 passengers were from the religious congregation. Other Pilgrims were "**merchant** adventurers." They hoped to become rich in America. Though some men left their families at home, others brought their wives and children with them.

Some of the passengers had no choice about making the voyage. Eighteen passengers were servants. Some were **indentured servants**. That means they had been "sold" to their owners for a fixed period of time, usually seven years. They weren't allowed to leave service until their contract was up.

The More Children

In the seventeenth century, children could be sold as indentured servants if they were homeless, from poor families, or if it was unclear who their parents were. The More family was wealthy, but the children's father claimed they were not his. The four children were taken from their mother and put on the *Mayflower* to be servants in America. Mary (age 4), Jasper (age 7), and Elinor (age 8) died in the first winter in the New World. But Richard (age 5 during the voyage) lived to be 81, and became a ship's captain.

The passengers were divided into two groups. Each had a nickname for the other. The adventurers called the religious people "Saints." The passengers sailing for religious reasons called the others "Strangers." Sometimes there were conflicts between the two groups. Though the Saints were fewer in number, they wanted all of the other passengers to follow their religious rules. These rules were usually very strict. The Strangers and the crew had no interest in following the Saints' religion.

Though the passengers were very different, they signed the Mayflower Compact, agreeing to work together.

Mayflower by the Numbers

The *Mayflower* started with 102 passengers. Two people died on the trip across the ocean. One baby was born. His parents named him Oceanus. About half of the Pilgrims died in their first winter in the New World.

Passengers on the *Mayflower* included religious separatists, as well as merchants, farmers, servants, and families.

Chapter 3
A Two-Month Voyage

Life on the *Mayflower* was crowded, smelly, and dangerous. The journey took over two months to complete. Most passengers were seasick for the first few weeks, even though the seas were calm. Strong storms struck in the second half of the voyage. The ship almost wrecked when an important support beam broke. Two people died along the way.

There was not a lot of space on the *Mayflower*. Everyone lived close together. They slept, ate, and used the bathroom close to each other. There were no toilets, only buckets. The buckets were out in the open or behind a sheet. They often spilled if the ship hit a big wave.

The ship had levels, called decks. The Pilgrims lived on the gun deck. The main deck was where the crew worked and the captain steered the ship. There was also a deck for supplies. To get from the gun deck to the main deck, the passengers had to climb a rope or a ladder. In good weather they could get fresh air on the main deck. If the seas were rough, they had to stay below. The crew worried they would be washed overboard.

Passengers did not only have bad weather to face. People also got sick. The passengers didn't have fresh fruits or vegetables once they left England, so some passengers got scurvy. Scurvy is a disease that comes from a lack of vitamin C. It causes bleeding gums, weakness, and even death.

The ship carried all the food they would need for the voyage. It also had extra food to help them when they landed in the New World. Some of the food included salt pork, dried fish, oats, pickles, cheese,

Hardtack lasted a long time but was hard enough to break teeth, and got infested with beetles.

and a kind of bland cracker called **hardtack**. Hardtack usually had to be soaked in water before it could be eaten. By the end of the voyage, some hardtack was infested with beetles.

It was not common to drink water on the journey. Instead, children and adults drank beer. Water either ran out or got dirty on the journey. However, the alcohol in beer made it safe to drink. People drank beer with every meal. It was not good for children to drink it so often, though. Some got sick.

A Child's Day on the *Mayflower*

6 a.m.	Wake up
6:30 a.m.	Go to the bathroom in a bucket, behind a sheet
7 a.m.	Eat breakfast—oatmeal, dried cow tongue, and beer
8 a.m.-12 p.m.	Play games, sing, and stay out of the way of the crew
12 p.m.	Lunch—hardtack, cheese, and beer
1-7 p.m.	Rough seas, so passengers must stay below the main deck
7:30 p.m.	Dinner—dried fish stew, pickles, and beer
8 p.m.	Bedtime, on the floor or in a hammock

Because water often went bad, most of the passengers drank beer instead.

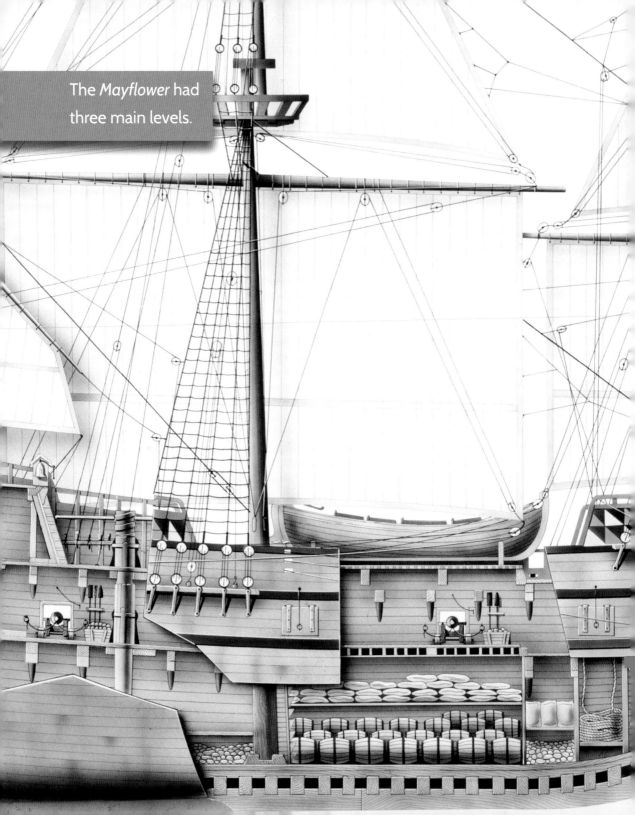

The *Mayflower* had three main levels.

Chapter 4

The *Mayflower*

The *Mayflower* was a merchant ship. It usually carried items to sell overseas. The *Mayflower* was about 100 feet (30.5 meters) long and about 25 feet (7.6 m) wide. The ship had been built fifteen years before the Pilgrims' voyage. That made it very old for a ship of that time.

The *Mayflower* was a sailing ship. It had three sails, called masts. On the deck were tall structures that helped protect the crew from wind and sea spray.

The *Mayflower* had three levels: the main deck, the gun deck, and the cargo hold. The main deck was on top. Some of it was in the open air, but there were also cabins. The captain had the biggest cabin,

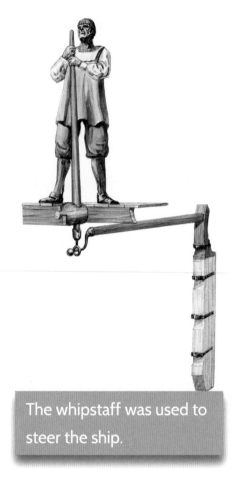

The whipstaff was used to steer the ship.

measuring 10 feet by 7 feet (3 m by 2 m). The **whipstaff**, which was used to steer instead of a wheel, was also on the main deck. The ship's kitchen was located at the very front of the main deck.

The second level was the gun deck. This was the passengers' main living space. They had to share it with the ship's weapons. The *Mayflower* had at least ten cannons on board. The biggest one was called a minion cannon. It weighed 1,200 pounds (544 kilograms) and fired a cannonball that weighed 3.5 pounds (1.5 kg). Also on that deck was the gun room, which held the gunpowder and assorted weapons. Passengers were not allowed in that room.

The bottom level was the cargo hold. It held all of the food and supplies needed for the voyage. It also had all of the passengers' personal belongings. They needed to take clothes, bedding, tools, weapons, and trading goods to their new home.

The *Mayflower* also carried several cannons.

Castles

Tall structures called castles helped protect the deck from the weather. However, the 30-foot (9 m) castles also slowed the *Mayflower* down. The western wind pushed against the castles and made the ship go slower. It took more than two months for the ship to make the journey. Going the other way, though, the castles helped the ship. The western wind pushed the *Mayflower* back to England in about one month.

It was a terribly cold winter when the Pilgrims landed.

Chapter 5

Remembering the *Mayflower* Today

The *Mayflower* reached land on November 9, 1620, at what is now Cape Cod, Massachusetts. However, life was hard for the Pilgrims when they arrived. This part of the New World had cold and snowy winters. The Pilgrims were not prepared. They spent most of the first winter living on the *Mayflower*.

About half of the Pilgrims died within a few months. The scurvy that developed on the voyage continued on land. Many also caught illnesses like pneumonia or **tuberculosis**. By spring, only 53 of the original 102 passengers who survived the trip were still alive. These Pilgrims built a small village, which they named Plymouth Colony. They placed six cannons

When the Pilgrims won the good will of the Native Americans, they began to prosper.

around it. After that first deadly winter, the colonists met the Native Americans of the area. They formed good relationships with the Native people. The Native Americans helped the Pilgrims survive.

Plymouth Colony was the first large English settlement in the New England region. In November 1621, a second ship of Pilgrims arrived. Other ships followed. By 1630, there were about three hundred people in the colony. In 1643, there were approximately two thousand people. Plymouth Colony later merged with the Massachusetts Bay Colony.

The passengers of the *Mayflower* left a lasting legacy in the land that became the United States of America. Today, there are many displays in museums that talk about the Pilgrims and the *Mayflower*.

Glossary

congregation A group of people gathered for religious worship.

hardtack A dry biscuit or cracker made from flour, water, and salt, used for long sea voyages.

indentured servant A person who worked for a number of years without pay, often in exchange for passage to another country or colony.

merchant A person involved in the selling and buying of goods and services.

Pilgrim One of the English colonists who settled in Plymouth; generally a person who travels for a religious reason.

tuberculosis A disease that damages the lungs and can cause death.

whipstaff A device used to control a ship's direction.

Find Out More

Books

Cook, Peter. *You Wouldn't Want to Sail on the Mayflower! A Trip That Took Entirely Too Long.* Danbury, CT: Franklin Watts, 2013.

Lynch, P. J. *The Boy Who Fell Off the Mayflower, or John Howland's Good Fortune.* Somerville, MA: Candlewick, 2015.

McGovern, Ann. *If You Sailed on the Mayflower in 1620.* New York: Scholastic, 2014.

Website

The First Thanksgiving
www.scholastic.com/scholastic_thanksgiving

Video

Tour of the *Mayflower II*
www.youtube.com/watch?v=ppDw52cWWtQ

Index

Page numbers in **boldface** are illustrations. Entries in **boldface** are glossary terms.

About the Author

Laura L. Sullivan is the author of more than thirty fiction and nonfiction books for children, including the fantasies *Under the Green Hill* and *Guardian of the Green Hill*. She has written many books for Cavendish Square, including *Life As a Cowboy in the American West*, *Life As a Spy in the American Revolution*, *Life As an Explorer with Lewis and Clark*, and *Life As a Child in a Japanese Internment Camp*.